DISNEY CLASSIC S̶ONG̶S

ISBN-13: 978-1-4234-1276-2
ISBN-10: 1-4234-1276-1

Wonderland Music Company, Inc.

Walt Disney Music Company

7777 W. BLUEMOUND RD. P.O. BOX 13819 MILWAUKEE, WI 53213

The following songs are the property of:
Bourne Co.
Music Publishers
5 West 37th Street
New York, NY 10018

WHEN I SEE AN ELEPHANT FLY
WHEN YOU WISH UPON A STAR
WITH A SMILE AND A SONG

ON THE CD . . .

Julian Brightman
Julian has sung from Broadway to the White House, and all points in between. Career highlights include *Peter Pan* and *Hello, Dolly!* on Broadway; *West Side Story* at the legendary La Scala Opera House in Milan; and *The Fantasticks* at Washington, D.C.'s historic Ford's Theatre.

Sarah Jane Everman
Sarah has appeared at the New York City Center with the Encores series. She has performed on Broadway in *Wicked, Wonderful Town,* and *The Apple Tree.*

Susan Derry
Susan has performed on Broadway in *Wonderful Town* (Eileen) and *The Phantom of the Opera* (Christine); and she has appeared as a guest soloist with the New York Pops at Carnegie Hall. She attended Northwestern University and received her Masters in Voice from the Manhattan School of Music.

Jeff Whiting
Jeff has originated numerous roles for Walt Disney Entertainment, including Quasimodo in Disneyworld's *Hunchback of Notre Dame*, and Peter Pan and Young Hercules aboard the Disney Magic, as a member of the original cast of the Disney Cruise Line's inaugural season. Jeff currently serves as Assistant Director to the National Tours of *Hairspray* and *The Producers.*

Producer **Michael Dansicker** has worked as arranger, composer, musical director and pianist on over 100 Broadway and Off-Broadway productions; from *Grease* (1975) to *Series of Dreams* (Tharp/Dylan Project '05.) His musical *Twenty Fingers, Twenty Toes* (Book, Music and Lyrics) has been performed Off-Broadway at the NY WPA Theatre and The York and his Boogie-Woogie Opera *Swing Shift* was performed at the Manhattan Theatre Club. He has composed original music for over a dozen plays in New York, including The *Glass Menagerie* (revival with Jessica Tandy) and *Total Abandon* (with Richard Dreyfus), and musically supervised the Royal Shakespeare Company transfers of *Piaf, Good,* and *Les Liasons Dangereuses.* He served as vocal consultant to the hit films *Elf* (New Line Cinema), *Analyze That!* (Warner Bros.), and *Meet the Parents* (Universal), and also scored the dance sequences for Paramount's comedy classic *Brain Donors* (starring John Turturro). In the world of concert dance, he has composed and scored pieces for Twyla Tharp, American Ballet Theatre, Geoffrey Holder, Mikhail Baryshnikov, and The Joffrey, as well as serving as pianist to Jerome Robbins and Agnes Demille. Michael currently works as creative consultant to Walt Disney Entertainment. For Hal Leonard Corporation, he composed the music for *The Audition Suite* (lyrics by Martin Charnin) and compiled the four books of The *16-Bar Theatre Audition* series. As a vocal coach, he works with the top talent in New York and Hollywood (including Sony's pop division). As audition pianist, he works regularly with important casting directors on both coasts, and for 15 years has played all major auditions for Jay Binder, the "dean" of Broadway casting. Mr. Dansicker's original music is licensed by BMI. He holds a MA from the Catholic University of America.

CONTENTS

Singers on the CD:
Julian Brightman (tracks 1, 10), **Sarah Jane Everman** (tracks 3, 6),
Susan Derry (track 9), **Jeff Whiting** (tracks 2, 4, 5, 7, 8)

Pianists on the CD:
Ruben Piirainen (1, 4, 10, 11, 14, 20), Hank Powell (2, 3, 5-9, 12, 13, 15-19)

Vocal Tracks produced by Michael Dansicker
Engineered by Chip Fabrizi at P.P.I. Recording, Inc., New York City

4

THE BARE NECESSITIES

from Walt Disney's *The Jungle Book*

Words and Music by
Terry Gilkyson

To Coda

fond - er _____ of my big home.
raw paw, _____ well, next time, be - ware.

The bees are buzz - ing in the tree _____ to make some

hon - ey, just _____ for me. When you look un - der the

rocks and plants, take a glance at the fan - cy ants _____ and may - be try a few! _____

The bare ne - ces - si - ties of life will come to you, _

_ will come to you. _____

D.S. al Coda

CODA

Don't pick the

prick - ly pear ____ by the paw; when you pick a pear, ____

____ try to use the claw, ____ but you don't need to

use the claw ____ when you pick a pear of the big paw - paw.

CANDLE ON THE WATER

from Walt Disney's *Pete's Dragon*

Words and Music by Al Kasha
and Joel Hirschhorn

I'll be your can-dle on the wa-ter, my love for you will al-ways
I'll be your can-dle on the wa-ter 'til ev-'ry wave is warm and

burn. I know you're lost and drift-ing, but the clouds are lift-ing.
bright. My soul is there be-side you, let this can-dle guide you;

Don't give up; you have some-where to turn.
soon you'll see a gold-en stream of light.

A DREAM IS A WISH
YOUR HEART MAKES
from Walt Disney's *Cinderella*

Words and Music by Mack David,
Al Hoffman and Jerry Livingston

THE LORD IS GOOD TO ME

from Walt Disney's *Melody Time*

Words and Music by Kim Gannon
and Walter Kent

*The singer may choose to leave off the last "me" and whistle only.

THE SECOND STAR TO THE RIGHT
from Walt Disney's *Peter Pan*

Words by Sammy Cahn
Music by Sammy Fain

SO THIS IS LOVE
(The Cinderella Waltz)
from Walt Disney's *Cinderella*

Words and Music by Mack David,
Al Hoffman and Jerry Livingston

WHEN I SEE AN ELEPHANT FLY

from Walt Disney's *Dumbo*

Words by Ned Washington
Music by Oliver Wallace

WITH A SMILE AND A SONG

from Walt Disney's *Snow White and the Seven Dwarfs*

Words by Larry Morey
Music by Frank Churchill

D.S. al Coda

CODA

With a smile and a song.

fill the world with sun - shine. When you smile and you

sing, Ev - 'ry thing is in tune and it's spring and

life flows a - long, With a smile and a song.

WHEN YOU WISH UPON A STAR
from Walt Disney's *Pinocchio*

Words by Ned Washington
Music by Leigh Harline

ZIP-A-DEE-DOO-DAH
from Walt Disney's *Song of the South*

Words by Ray Gilbert
Music by Allie Wrubel

About the Enhanced CD

In addition to full performances and piano accompaniments playable on both your CD player and computer, this enhanced CD also includes tempo adjustment and transposition software for computer use only. This software, known as the Amazing Slow Downer, was originally created for use in pop music to allow singers and players the freedom to independently adjust both tempo and pitch elements. Because we believe there may be valuable educational use for these features in classical and theatre music, we have included this software as a tool for both the teacher and student. For quick and easy installation instructions of this software please see below.

This new software feature allows you to adjust the tempo up and down without affecting the pitch. Likewise, the Amazing Slow Downer allows you to shift pitch up and down without affecting the tempo. We recommend that these new tempo and pitch adjustment features be used with care and insight. Ideally, you will be using these recorded accompaniments and the Amazing Slow Downer for practice only.

The audio quality may be somewhat compromised when played through the Amazing Slow Downer. This compromise in quality will not be a factor in playing the CD audio track on a normal CD player or through another audio computer program.

Installation instructions for the Amazing Slow Downer software:

For Macintosh OS 8, 9 and X:
- Load the CD-ROM into your CD-ROM Drive on your computer.
- Each computer is set up a little differently. Your computer may automatically open the audio CD portion of this enhanced CD and begin to play it.
- Double-click on the data portion of the CD-ROM (which will have the Hal Leonard icon in red and be named as the book).
- Double-click on the "Amazing OS 8 (9 or X)" folder.
- Double-click "Amazing Slow Downer"/"Amazing X PA" to run the software from the CD-ROM, or copy this file to your hard disk and run it from there.
- Follow the instructions on-screen to get started. The Amazing Slow Downer should display tempo, pitch and mix bars. Click to select your track and adjust pitch or tempo by sliding the appropriate bar to the left or to the right.

For Windows:
- Load the CD-ROM into your CD-ROM Drive on your computer.
- Each computer is set up a little differently. Your computer may automatically open the audio CD portion of this enhanced CD and begin to play it.
- To access the CD-ROM features, click on My Computer then right click on the Drive that you placed the CD in. Click Open. You should then see a folder named "Amazing Slow Downer". Click to open the "Amazing Slow Downer" folder.
- Double-click "setup.exe" to install the software from the CD-ROM to your hard disk. Follow the on-screen instructions to complete installation.
- Go to "Start", "Programs" and find the "Amazing Slow Downer" folder. Go to that folder and select the "Amazing Slow Downer" software.
- Follow the instructions on-screen to get started. The Amazing Slow Downer should display tempo, pitch and mix bars. Click to select your track and adjust pitch or tempo by sliding the appropriate bar to the left or to the right.
- Note: On Windows NT, 2000 and XP, the user should be logged in as the "Administrator" to guarantee access to the CD-ROM drive. Please see the help file for further information.

Minimum system requirements:

For Macintosh:
Power Macintosh; Mac OS 8.5 or higher; 4 MB Application RAM; 8x Multi-Session CD-ROM drive

For Windows:
Pentium Processor; Windows 95, 98, ME, NT, 2000, XP; 4 MB Application RAM; 8x Multi-Session CD-ROM drive